A Note to Parents and Teachers

DK READERS is a compelling reading programme for children, designed in conjunction with leading literacy experts, including Cliff Moon M.Ed., Honorary Fellow of the University of Reading. Cliff Moon has spent many years as a teacher and teacher educator specializing in reading and has written more than 140 books for children and teachers. He reviews regularly for teachers' journals.

Beautiful illustrations and superb full-colour photographs combine with engaging, easy-to-read stories to offer a fresh approach to each subject in the series. Each DK READER is guaranteed to capture a child's interest while developing his or her reading skills, general knowledge, and love of reading.

The five levels of DK READERS are aimed at different reading abilities, enabling you to choose the books that are exactly right for your child:

Pre-level 1 – Learning to read
Level 1 – Beginning to read
Level 2 – Beginning to read alone
Level 3 – Reading alone
Level 4 – Proficient readers

The "normal" age at which a child begins to read can be anywhere from three to eight years old, so these levels are only a general guideline.

No matter which level you select, you can be sure that you are helping your child learn to read, then read to learn!

D0319138

DK

LONDON, NEW YORK, MUNICH,
MELBOURNE AND DELHI

Senior Art Editor Cheryl Telfer
Designer Sadie Thomas
Series Editor Deborah Lock
Production Shivani Pandey
Picture Researcher
Sarah Stewart-Richardson
DTP Designer Almudena Díaz
Jacket Designer Chris Drew

Reading Consultant
Cliff Moon, M.Ed.

Published in Great Britain by Dorling Kindersley Limited
80, The Strand, London WC2R 0RL

8 10 9 7

A Penguin Company

Copyright © 2004 Dorling Kindersley Limited, London

A CIP record for this book is
available from the British Library

ISBN-13: 978-0-7513-6794-2

Colour reproduction by Colourscan, Singapore
Printed and bound in China by L Rex Printing Co., Ltd.

The publisher would like to thank the following for
their kind permission to reproduce their images:
Position key: c=centre; b=bottom; l=left; r=right; t=top
Getty Images: Anup Shah 1, John Giustina 6-7, Tim Flach 6tr,
Jeff Hunter 14, 16, Paul Souders 18, Eastcott Momatiuk 28-29;
Corbis: Wolfgang Kaehler 3, Lynda Richardson 8, Jeffrey L.
Rotman, 21t, W. Perry Conway 21c, 32tl, Robert Pickett 28b,
Renee Lynn 30-31, Buddy Mays 31t, Kevin Schafer 32cr;
N.H.P.A.: Stephen Dalton 4-5, 6tl, Linda Pitkin 14-15, Keven
Schafer, 21b; **Alamy Images:** Chris Caldicott 5r, Steve Bloom 32bl;
DK Picture Library: Jerry Young 9cr, 10, 11c, 27t, Drusillas Zoo
23t, Philip Dowell 28c; **Ecoscene:** Lando Pescatori 13b, Visual &
Written 20; **Nature Picture Library Ltd:** Jeff Rotman 15c, Peter
Blackwell 30t, Brandon Cole 30c;

All other images © Dorling Kindersley Limited
For further information see: www.dkimages.com

See our complete catalogue at

www.dk.com

Feathers, flippers and feet

Written by Deborah Lock

A Dorling Kindersley Book

All around the world, there are animals moving – flying in the air, crawling on land or swimming in the oceans.

Animals move to catch food.

Animals move
to explore their
environment.

Animals move to
escape danger.

Take a closer look
at the different ways
animals move and discover
some unusual tricks.

Wings are for flying
high in the air.
Wings are for preening,
parading and flapping.

Wings are for swooping,
SOARING and
gliding.

Wings are for darting, flitting and fluttering.

Wings are for catching the *breeze.*

Whose feathers are these?

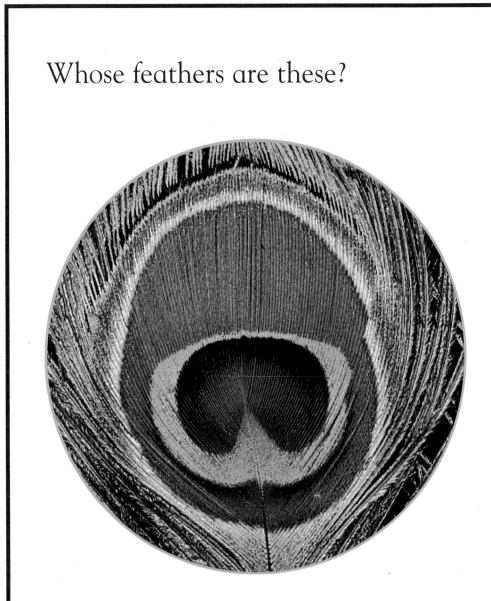

He struts proudly around and
has a long, colourful train
that he can raise like a fan.

She swoops silently on her prey at night.

His graceful feathers are soft and white.

His colourful feathers are very bright.

Flying high

To fly, birds not only flap their wings, but also open and close the gaps between their feathers.

Were you right? Let's find out.

A peacock shows off his colourful feathers to attract a mate.

The soft feathers of the barn owl are shaped to muffle the sound of her wing beats.

A swan is born with grey feathers, which gradually turn to snowy white.

Parrot feathers contain chemicals that reflect the light to give them amazing colours.

Not all wings are made of feathers.

Amazingly, a bumblebee's small, fine wings can lift its heavy body.

Buzzzzzzzz

How do bees fly?

Bees do not flap their wings, but flip them forwards and backwards to create a lifting effect.

When a leaf butterfly closes its wings, it looks just like a leaf — a perfect disguise!

Can you see it?

A ladybird has another pair of wings underneath its red, spotted pair.

Flippers are for
swimming through
the water.

Flippers are for
leaping, swirling
and splashing.

Flippers are for dodging,
dashing and chasing.

Flippers are for paddling,
flipping and rolling.
Flippers are for darting away.

Whose flippers are these?

An ocean giant is on a long trip.
He spends winter in the Caribbean
and summer in the Arctic.

Her long front flippers provide her with speed.

He waddles on land, but swims with ease.

Look carefully at this one – it's a trick.

Flippers and fins

Flippers are the arm bones of ocean mammals. Fins are not supported by bones.

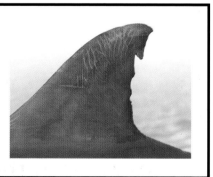

Were you right? Let's find out.

A humpback whale has the longest
flippers of any animal.

A sea lion has two pairs
of flippers that help
her move quickly on
land and in water.

A penguin is a flightless
bird whose wings
are used as
flippers.

A diver wears flippers
to swim down into
deep water to
explore a wreck or
an underwater cave.

Ocean mammals can also use
their flippers to do other things.

A manatee uses its flippers to hold
on to its food.

A dolphin uses its flippers to make friendly contact with its babies.

A seal uses its flippers to push itself forwards on land.

Burying eggs

Each year, sea turtles visit the same beach to lay their eggs. They use their flippers to bury them in the sand.

Feet are for moving
around on land.

Feet are for running,
jumping and
leaping.

Feet are for
walking,
waddling
and sliding.

Feet are for climbing, clinging and grasping.

Feet are for scampering away.

Whose feet are these?

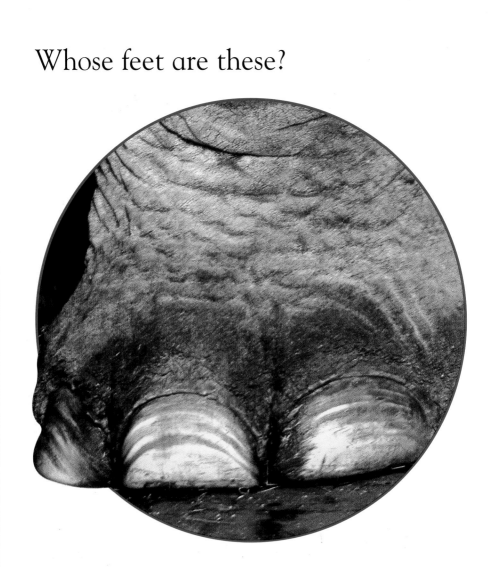

He is the heaviest animal on land.
He uses his great big feet
to loosen the plants he eats
because he has no hands.

He's a small tropical lizard who can walk across a ceiling.

You'll find her in the water quacking, splashing and swimming.

He gets bigger and bigger because he is always eating.

Were you right? Let's find out.
An elephant spreads his huge
weight across his four feet.

A gecko's feet are covered with tiny hairs, which help him to slide along any surface without slipping.

"Quack!"

When swimming, a duckling uses her webbed feet like paddles.

A caterpillar has feet that are like suckers with small claws on the end for gripping the leaves he's eating.

What else can animals do with their feet?

A tree frog has suckers on its feet that stick to any surface.

A water boatman can float on water by spreading out its feet.

Birds of prey catch food with their clawed feet, which are called talons.

Dogs use their paws to scratch an itch.

Who holds the records?

A Ruppell's Griffon vulture
was flying at 11,277 metres
(37,000 feet) when it
hit an aeroplane.

The sperm
whale makes the
deepest dives of
any animal.

The slowest
mammal is the
three-toed
sloth, who spends
most of the day
hanging from branches asleep.

When chasing its prey, a cheetah
can reach speeds of 105 kilometres
per hour (65 miles per hour).

Fascinating facts

The wandering albatross
has the longest wingspan
of any bird.

A butterfly uses its feet
to taste whether food
is good enough to eat.

Although an ostrich has
fluffy feathers, it cannot
fly. Instead, it struts
on long legs.

Unlike monkeys, the sifaka
has to bounce as if it were on
a trampoline because its arms
are shorter than its legs.

A walrus has rough, thick
skin on the bottom of its
flippers to grip when it
moves on rocks or ice.

When they are angry,
rhinos can charge faster
than an Olympic sprinter.